D0128609

# Burgoyne Surrounded Quilt

## by

## Eleanor Burns

From the Quilt in a Day® Series

To Grant

Published by Quilt in a Day, Inc.
1955 Diamond Street
San Marcos, Ca 92069

Copyright © 1992 by Eleanor Burns
First Printing, April, 1992
ISBN 0-922705-36-4
Design and Layout, Quilt in a Day Art Dept.
Photography, Wayne Norton

# Table of Contents

# Historical Significance

The Burgoyne Surrounded Quilt is named after a British General, John Burgoyne, the gentleman credited with losing America during the American Revolution.

The quilt pattern depicts an actual battle from the American Revolution. The chains of small squares represent regiments of Redcoats from the British armies of Burgoyne, marching from Canada, and General Howe, marching from New York. The circle represents militiamen from New England, surrounding Burgoyne in Saratoga, New York, represented by the large center.

In June of 1777, 7000 British soldiers gathered in Canada under "Gentleman Johnny" Burgoyne, a poetry-writing, party-loving British general. He planned to end the war by moving his Redcoats down from Canada to Albany, sealing New England off from the southern colonies. There he would be met by Redcoats sent north from New York by General Howe. Enraged, blue clad American colonists from New England swarmed around Burgoyne like "birds of prey" at Saratoga. Four days later Burgoyne surrendered his entire force. Worse, General Howe never sent the promised help from New York, but instead left for Philadelphia. Saratoga proved to be the turning point of the war, because it convinced France to become America's ally.

After we won the Revolution, and were no longer under British rule, it was natural that American quiltmakers preferred to call the very same pattern Road to California. A traveling quiltmaker with imagination could easily see the crisscrossing trails and wagon wheels depicted in the pieces on the quilt.

Those fortunate enough to make their way westward in sturdy Conestoga wagons referred to the graphic quilt pattern as Homestead or Homespun. Perhaps the large central block once representing the capture at Saratoga, now represented happy homesteads, with wagon traveled trails between them.

# Introduction

In 1775, a society of patriotic ladies at Edenton, North Carolina, pledged to drink no more tea until justice was done in America. Several colonial newspapers carried this poem, reading in part:

*No more shall my teapot so generous be*

*In filling the cups with this pernicious tea,*

*For I'll fill it with water and drink out the same,*

*Before I'll lose Liberty that dearest name.*

What followed is a familiar part of our country's history, with women giving up their beloved sons and husbands in the name of peace and union. A captured British soldier at the battle of Saratoga described these intense men with these words:

*"Not one of the Americans was regularly equipped. But the determination which caused them to grasp a musket and powder-horn can be seen in their faces, as well as that they are not to be fooled with, especially in skirmishes in the woods."*

In bonding with the women of the American Revolution, I proudly dedicate Burgoyne Surrounded to my older son, Grant, a young man devoted to peace and unity.

We are much the same as the countrywomen of yesteryear — conscious of the struggle for freedom, anxious for the well-being of our men, and creative with our hands. Just as the "minutemen were at the ready," I'm prepared to quilt at a moment's notice. I do enjoy sewing on my five-thread serger, whizzing down fabric strips, slicing them into segments, and zipping them back into colorful patches. Burgoyne Surrounded allows the luxury of speedy strip sewing, and freedom from tedious squaring of pieced triangles. Even through I prefer to "speed sew" the Burgoyne Surrounded quilt on a serger, you, too, may savor each moment if sewing on a conventional machine. We both can enjoy the peace derived from working with cotton fabric, color, and design.

Burgoyne Surrounded is a perfect "gentleman's quilt," with its strong graphic design and interesting historical background. A one-block wallhanging can be a striking addition to a professional office. As Paul Revere's cry resounded through the countryside, this quilt cries out for a red, white, and blue color selection. Others may choose contemporary red, black and grey. But the quilt can also be feminine, depending on the fabric choice and bedroom setting. Whatever your taste, Burgoyne Surrounded is an easy and enjoyable quilt to make.

May your sorrows be patched, and your joys be quilted.

*Eleanor Burns*

# About the Burgoyne Block and Connecting Cornerstones and Lattices

The size of one block is approximately 23" square. It is made with six different patches, each sewn or cut from strips.

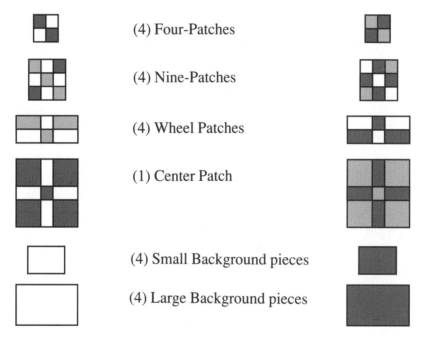

(4) Four-Patches

(4) Nine-Patches

(4) Wheel Patches

(1) Center Patch

(4) Small Background pieces

(4) Large Background pieces

After the blocks are made, they are set together with two other pieces.

Cornerstones

Lattice strips

Borders are added to complete the quilt top.

# Fabric Selection

## The Background:

The Background can be either light or dark. Since it dominates three fourths of the quilt, be careful in your selection that it is not too bright or overbearing.

Select a small scale print, a print that appears solid from a distance, or a "marbleized" fabric. Do not use a directional or one-way print.

## The Trail:

The Trail is the "X" across the block. It is made from the Four-Patch, the Center Patch, and pieces within the Nine-Patch.

The same fabric is used in the Cornerstone with the Lattice between or around blocks.

Select a small or medium scale print, or a fabric that appears solid from a distance. A large floral print may also be used, featured particularly in the Center Patch.

## The Wheel:

The Wheel is the circle within the block. It is made from the Wheel Patch and pieces within the Nine-Patch.

Select a small or medium scale print, or a fabric that appears solid from a distance.

# Making a Quilt with a Light Background:

You may soften a Light Background by using a pastel print. If you choose a Light Background, select the Trail fabric from one color family, and the Wheel fabric from a second color family.

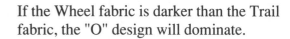

If the Trail fabric is darker than the Wheel fabric, the "X" design will dominate.

If the Wheel fabric is darker than the Trail fabric, the "O" design will dominate.

If the Trail fabric and the Wheel fabric are of equal value against a Light Background, a strong graphic design is created.

# Making a Quilt with a Dark Background:

Select a light fabric for the Trail. The same light may also be used as the Wheel fabric. When purchasing fabric, total the yardage for the Trail and the Wheel.

Or you may choose a second light or a medium.

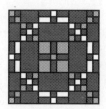

Antique quilts were often made with two solid fabrics: Turkey Red and muslin or Confederate Blue and muslin.

# Baby Quilt

You may make copies of this page for design purposes.

Color in a representation of your fabric selection with pencils or crayons.

Approximate Size: 41" x 41"

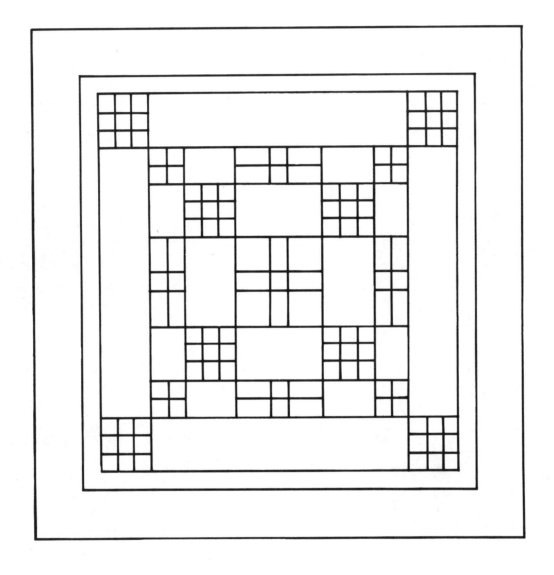

# Yardage and Cutting for Baby Quilt

| **Trail** 3/8 yd. | **Wheel** 1/3 yd. | **Background** 1 yd. |
|---|---|---|
| Paste in fabric swatch | Paste in fabric swatch | Paste in fabric swatch |
| Cut (3) 2" x 44" strips | Cut (2) 2" x 44" strips | Cut (4) 2" x 44" strips |

## Additional Yardage and Cutting

| | |
|---|---|
| **First Border** | **Wheel**  1/3 yd. |
| | Cut (4) 2" x 44" strips |
| **Second Border** | **Trail**  2/3 yd. |
| | Cut (4) 4 1/2" x 44" strips |
| **Backing** | **Light**  1 1/4 yds. |
| **Batting** | 48" x 48" |
| **Binding\*** | 1/2 yd. |
| | Cut (5) 3" x 44" strips |

\*for Machine Quilted Finish Only

# Lap Quilt

You may make copies of this page for design purposes.

Color in a representation of your fabric selection with pencils or crayons.

Approximate Size:   41" x 68"

# Yardage and Cutting for Lap Quilt

| Trail 1/2 yd. | Wheel 3/8 yd. | Background 1 3/4 yd. |
|---|---|---|
| Paste in fabric swatch | Paste in fabric swatch | Paste in fabric swatch |
| Cut (5) 2" x 44" strips | Cut (4) 2" x 44" strips | Cut (8) 2" x 44" strips |

## Additional Yardage and Cutting

| | |
|---|---|
| **First Border** | **Wheel** 1/2 yd. |
| | Cut (6) 2" x 44" strips |
| **Second Border** | **Trail** 1 yd. |
| | Cut (7) 4 1/2" x 44" strips |
| **Backing** | **Light** 2 1/8 yds. |
| **Batting** | 45" x 76" |
| **Binding*** | 2/3 yd. |
| | Cut (7) 3" x 44" strips |

*for Machine Quilted Finish Only

# Twin Quilt

You may make copies of this page for design purposes.

Color in a representation of your fabric selection with pencils or crayons.  The Coverlet has two borders.

The Bedspread has three borders.

Approximate Size:    Coverlet   67" x 94"          Bedspread   79" x 106"

# Yardage and Cutting for Twin Quilt

| Trail    1 yd. | Wheel    7/8 yd. | Background    4 yds. |
|---|---|---|
| Paste in fabric swatch | Paste in fabric swatch | Paste in fabric swatch |
| Cut (10) 2" x 44" strips | Cut (10) 2" x 44" strips | Cut (19) 2" x 44" strips |

## Additional Yardage and Cutting

| | Coverlet | Bedspread |
|---|---|---|
| First Border | Wheel  5/8 yd. <br> Cut (7) 2" x 44" strips | Wheel  5/8 yd. <br> Cut (7) 2" x 44" strips |
| Second Border | Trail   1 1/4 yds. <br> Cut (8) 4 1/2" x 44" strips | Background 1 1/4 yds. <br> Cut (8) 4 1/2" x 44" strips |
| Third Border | | Trail 2 yds. <br> Cut (10) 6 1/2" x 44" strips |
| Backing | Light  6 yds. <br> Cut (2) equal pieces | Light  6 1/2 yds. <br> Cut (2) equal pieces |
| Batting | 70" x 96" | 86" x 110" |
| Binding* | 7/8 yd. <br> Cut (9) 3" x 44" strips | 1 yd. <br> Cut (10) 3" x 45" strips |

*for Machine Quilted Finish Only

# Double Quilt

You may make copies of this page for design purposes.

Color in a representation of your fabric selection with pencils or crayons.  The Coverlet has two borders.

The Bedspread has three borders.

Approximate Size:   Coverlet   72" x  98"        Bedspread 82" x 110"

# Yardage and Cutting for Double Quilt

| Trail 1 yd. | Wheel 7/8 yd. | Background 4 yds. |
|---|---|---|
| Paste in fabric swatch | Paste in fabric swatch | Paste in fabric swatch |
| Cut (10) 2" x 44" strips | Cut (10) 2" x 44" strips | Cut (19) 2" x 44" strips |

## Additional Yardage and Cutting

| | Coverlet | Bedspread |
|---|---|---|
| **First Border** | **Wheel** 5/8 yd. <br> Cut (7) 2" x 44" strips | **Wheel** 5/8 yd. <br> Cut (7) 2" x 44" strips |
| **Second Border** | **Trail** 1 1/2 yds. <br> Cut (8) 6 1/2" x 44" strips | **Background** 1 1/4 yds. <br> Cut (8) 4 1/2" x 44" strips |
| **Third Border** | | **Trail** 2 3/4 yds. <br> Cut (10) 8 1/2" x 44" strips |
| **Backing** | **Light** 6 1/2 yds. <br> Cut (2) equal pieces | **Light** 9 1/2 yds. <br> Cut (3) equal pieces |
| **Batting** | 86" x 110" | 96" x 120" |
| **Binding*** | 1 yd. <br> Cut (9) 3" x 44" strips | 1 yd. <br> Cut (10) 3" x 45" strips |

*for Machine Quilted Finish Only

# Queen Quilt

You may make copies of this page for design purposes.

Color in a representation of your fabric selection with pencils or crayons.  The Coverlet has two borders.

The Bedspread has three borders.

Approximate Size:   Coverlet   93" x 93"          Bedspread   99" x 99"

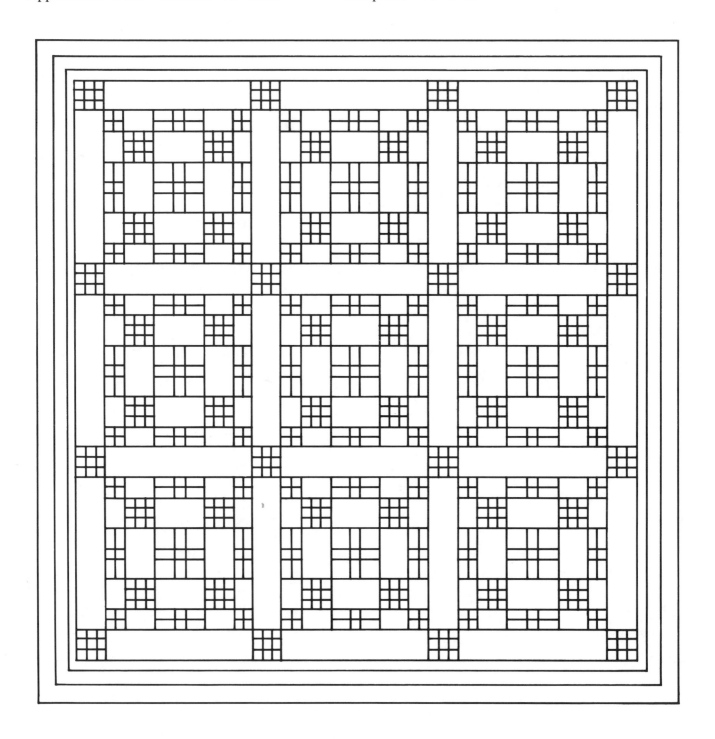

# Yardage and Cutting for Queen Quilt

| Trail  1 1/4 yds. | Wheel  1 1/8 yds. | Background  5 1/2 yds. |
|---|---|---|
| Paste in fabric swatch | Paste in fabric swatch | Paste in fabric swatch |
| Cut (13) 2" x 44" strips | Cut (14) 2" x 44" strips | Cut (25) 2" x 44" strips |

## Additional Yardage and Cutting

| | Coverlet | Bedspread |
|---|---|---|
| **First Border** | Wheel  3/4 yd.<br>Cut (9) 2" x 44" strips | Wheel  3/4 yd.<br>Cut (9) 2" x 44" strips |
| **Second Border** | Trail  1 1/4 yds.<br>Cut (9) 4 1/2" x 44" strips | Background  1 1/8 yds.<br>Cut (9) 3 1/2" x 44" strips |
| **Third Border** | | Trail  2 3/4 yds.<br>Cut (10) 4 1/2" x 44" strips |
| **Backing** | Light  8 1/2 yds.<br>Cut (3) equal pieces | Light  9 yds.<br>Cut (3) equal pieces |
| **Batting** | 98" x 98" | 108" x 108" |
| **Binding*** | 1 yd.<br>Cut (10) 3" x 44" strips | 1 1/8 yds.<br>Cut (11) 3" x 45" strips |

*for Machine Quilted Finish Only

# King Quilt

You may make copies of this page for design purposes.

Color in a representation of your fabric selection with pencils or crayons.  The Coverlet has two borders.

The Bedspread has three borders.

Approximate Size:    Coverlet    93" x  93"            Bedspread    105" x 105"

# Yardage and Cutting for King Quilt

**Trail     1 1/4 yds.**

| |
|:---:|
| Paste in fabric swatch |

Cut (13) 2" x 44" strips

**Wheel     1 1/8 yds.**

| |
|:---:|
| Paste in fabric swatch |

Cut (14) 2" x 44" strips

**Background   5 1/2 yds.**

| |
|:---:|
| Paste in fabric swatch |

Cut (25) 2" x 44" strips

## Additional Yardage and Cutting

| | Coverlet | Bedspread |
|---|---|---|
| **First Border** | **Wheel**  3/4 yd.<br>Cut (9) 2" x 44" strips | **Wheel**  3/4 yd.<br>Cut (9) 2" x 44" strips |
| **Second Border** | **Trail**  1 1/4 yds.<br>Cut (9) 4 1/2" x 44" strips | **Background**  1 1/4 yds.<br>Cut (9) 4 1/2" x 44" strips |
| **Third Border** | | **Trail**  2 yds.<br>Cut (10) 6 1/2" x 44" strips |
| **Backing** | **Light**  8 1/2 yds.<br>Cut (3) equal pieces | **Light**  9 1/2 yds.<br>Cut (3) equal pieces |
| **Batting** | 98" x 98" | 108" x 108" |
| **Binding\*** | 1 yd.<br>Cut (10) 3" x 44" strips | 1 1/8 yds.<br>Cut (11) 3" x 44" strips |

\*for Machine Quilted Finish Only

# Cutting Tools and Techniques

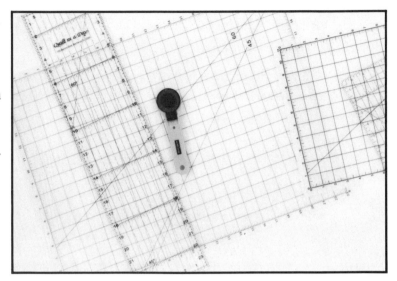

Use a large industrial size rotary cutter and fresh blade with a 6" x 24" ruler to cut strips. An 18" x 24" gridded cutting mat is adequate, however a 24" x 36" gridded cutting mat or larger is preferred. Work in an area large enough so that fabric or sewn strips never hang over the edge of the working table. Use a 6" x 12" ruler for conveniently cutting pieces from sewn strips. Use a 12 1/2" Square Up for carrying pieces from the cutting area to the sewing area.

Starting on page 10 refer to the Cutting Chart for your particular quilt size and setting.

## Cutting the Quilt Top Fabric into 2" Strips

*Begin with the Background fabric. This is the largest piece of yardage. Part of the Background fabric is cut into 2" strips, and the remainder of the fabric is cut after measuring pieces sewn from the 2" strips.*

1. Make a nick on the edge and tear from selvage to selvage to put the fabric on the straight-of-the-grain.

*To make cutting 2" Background strips more manageable, multiply the number of strips needed by 2", add 1" for straightening, and tear off that measurement of fabric. Proceed to cut the 2" strips from that fabric. Set the remaining Background fabric aside until pieces are sewn and measured.*

2. Fold the fabric in half, matching the torn straight edge thread to thread. It is often impossible to match the selvages.

3. Line up the torn edge of fabric on the gridded cutting mat with the left edge extended slightly to the left of zero. If you are confident in your cutting skills, layer Wheel fabric next, and Trail fabric on top. Once you cut the indicated number of 2" strips, remove that fabric from the stack.

4. Line up the 6" x 24" ruler on zero. Reverse this procedure if you are left-handed.

5. Spread the fingers of your left hand to hold the ruler firmly. With the rotary cutter in your right hand, begin cutting with the blade off the fabric on the mat. Put all your strength into the rotary cutter as you cut away from you, and trim the torn, ragged edge.

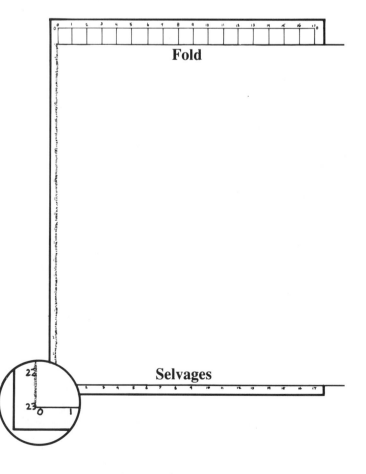

Fold

Selvages

6. Lift, and move your ruler over until it lines up with the 2" grid on the cutting mat. Cut the strip carefully and accurately.

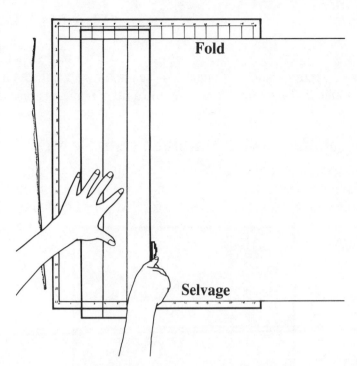

7. Lift the ruler, move it, and line it up with the 4" grid. Repeat, cutting as many 2" strips as indicated for your particular size quilt.

8. After cutting several strips, unfold and check to see that the strip is straight. If the strip is not straight, tear your fabric to put it on the straight-of-grain and begin again.

Additional wider strips are cut from the remaining Trail and Background fabrics as your sewing progresses and is measured.

## Cutting Strips in Halves and Fourths

Depending on your size quilt, only 1/2 or 1/4 of a strip may be needed.

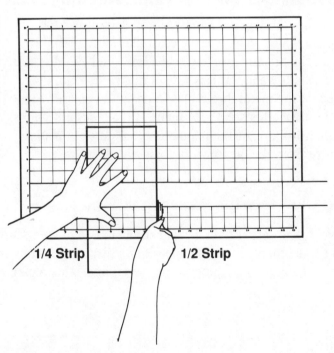

1. For 1/2 strip, fold the strip in half lengthwise, finger press a crease, open, and cut on the crease with a rotary cutter.

2. For 1/4 strip, fold the half strip in half again, crease, and rotary cut. Set the extra aside for later use.

## Cutting Border Strips

Use the 6" x 24" ruler and the grid lines on the cutting mat to cut each width for your size quilt.

# The 1/4" Seam

Sew an accurate and consistent 1/4" seam allowance throughout the sewing of the quilt. Do not change machines in the middle of making the quilt, because a consistent seam allowance is crucial.

## Conventional Sewing Machine Versus Serger

Burgoyne Surrounded can be made entirely on a conventional sewing machine. However, to speed the quilt making process, a serger can be used when making the top, as well as for a Quick Turn and Tie finish. A conventional machine is needed for a Machine Quilting and Binding finish.

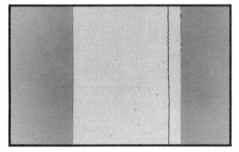
**Conventional seam**

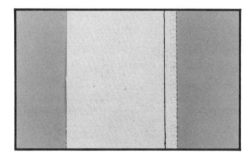
**Serger seam**

## Seam Allowance for Conventional Sewing Machine

The width of the presser foot usually determines the seam allowance. Line the edges of the fabric with the edge of the presser foot and sew a few stitches. Measure the seam allowance. If it is 1/4", a magnetic seam guide placed on the metal throat plate against the presser foot will assure a consistent 1/4" seam. If the measurement is less than 1/4", place the magnetic seam guide at a slight distance from the presser foot for a consistent seam.

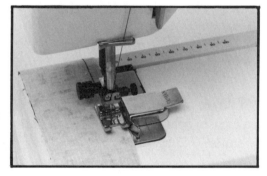

## Seam Allowance for Serger

A five thread serger with a chain stitch and an overcast stitch is preferred. If available, use the serger's fabric guide attachment, and make the seam adjustment by moving the guide. Do not let the serger's knife trim the edges. If a guide attachment is not available, stick a piece of moleskin to the serger so the seam is 1/4".

## Pressing

Use a steam iron on a gridded cushioned quilter's square, or ironing board.

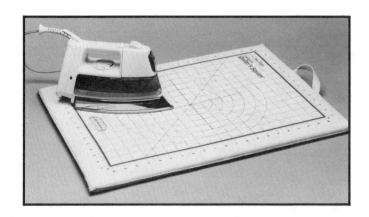

Light Background

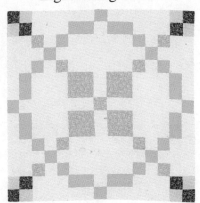

# The Four-Patch

**You need this many:**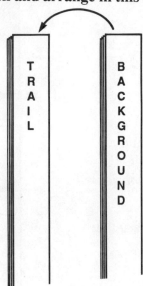

Baby . . . . . . . . . . . 4

Lap . . . . . . . . . . . 8

Twin . . . . . . . . . . 24

Double . . . . . . . . . 24

Queen . . . . . . . . . 36

King . . . . . . . . . . . 36

Dark Background

**Use the Trail Fabric and Background Fabric.**

## Making the Trail/Background

1. Count out 2" strips of **Trail** and **Background** fabrics.

**Stack and arrange in this order:**

TRAIL

BACKGROUND

**Stack this many strips:**

Baby . . . . . . 1/2 of each

Lap . . . . . . . . 1 of each

Twin . . . . . . . 3 of each

Double . . . . . 3 of each

Queen . . . . . . 4 of each

King . . . . . . . 4 of each

2. Flip the Background strip to the Trail strip, right sides together.

3. Set your machine with 15 stitches per inch, or 2 to 2.5 on machines with stitch selections from 1 to 4.

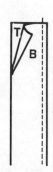

4. Line up the long edges. Sew a few inches with a 1/4" seam. Stop sewing and check the seam. Make an adjustment if necessary.

5. Assembly-line sew the strips together by butting one set of strips after the other without raising the presser foot or clipping the threads.

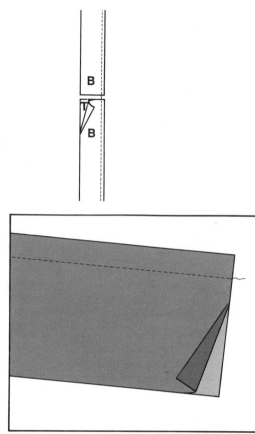

6. Drop the strips on the ironing board with the lighter strip on the bottom.

7. Press the seam to set it.

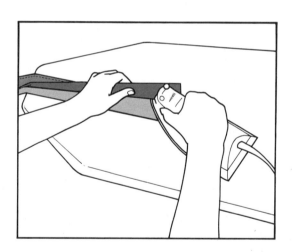

8. Lift up the darker strip on the top and press open. *This technique presses both seam allowances behind the dark fabric.*

9. Make certain that there are no folds at the seam line.

*Straight, pressed strips are essential for piecing accuracy. To avoid "bowed" strips use a cotton covered pressing mat ruled with a grid. The thick cushioned layer eliminates seam-edge impressions.*

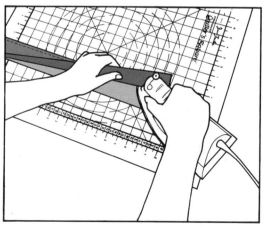

**If using a gridded pressing mat, line the strip with a grid.**

10. **Baby, Lap, Twin, and Double**

   Cut one sewn strip in half.

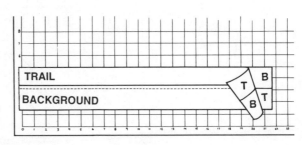

| BACKGROUND | |
|---|---|
| TRAIL | |

11. Place two sets of sewn strips right sides together on the cutting mat **with Trail fabric opposite each other.** Lock the seams by feeling along the seam allowance, pressing the layers to match. The strips must be the same width. *If they are not, check the seam or the pressing and redo as necessary.*

12. Line the strip with a straight line on the cutting mat and with the left end extended slightly to the left of zero.

13. With the 6" x 12" ruler and the rotary cutter, layer cut at zero to straighten the edge and remove the selvage.

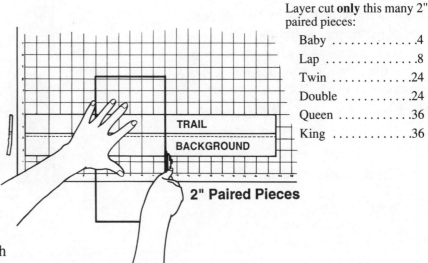

2" Paired Pieces

Layer cut **only** this many 2" paired pieces:

Baby . . . . . . . . . . . .4
Lap . . . . . . . . . . . . .8
Twin . . . . . . . . . . .24
Double . . . . . . . . . .24
Queen . . . . . . . . . .36
King . . . . . . . . . . .36

14. Lift the ruler, move it, and line it up with the 2" grid. Layer cut a pair.

15. Layer cut every 2", carefully lifting, moving, and lining up the ruler with the grid.

16. Carefully place the 2" paired pieces onto the Square Up or other ruler and carry them conveniently to the sewing machine.

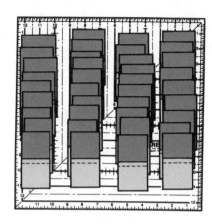

17. Wiggle-match the center seam.

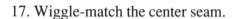

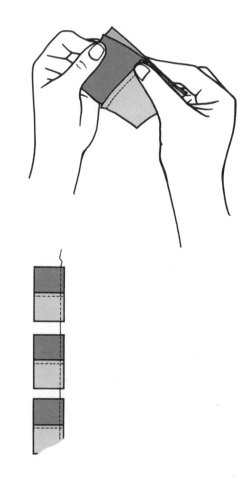

18. Assembly-line sew by butting one 2" paired piece after the other without raising the presser foot or cutting the threads. It is not necessary to backstitch.

19. Drop a string of Four-Patches on the pressing mat. Open and press from the right side.

20. Clip the connecting threads.

21. Measure several to find the average size.**Your Four-Patch measurement will be used when cutting the Wheel Patch and Background Piece. If the seam were a perfect 1/4", the Four-Patch would measure 3 1/2".** *However, seam allowances vary among sewing machines and sewers. Pressing techniques also make a difference.*

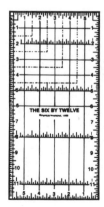

| B | T |
|---|---|
| T | B |

**Circle your measurement:
3 1/4"  3 3/8"  3 1/2"**

28

# The Wheel Patch

Light Background

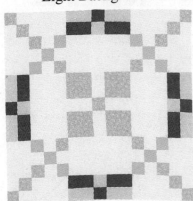

Dark Background

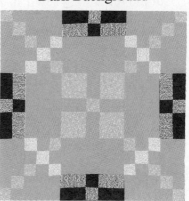

**You need this many:**

| Baby | ............ | 4 |
| Lap | ............ | 8 |
| Twin | ........... | 24 |
| Double | .......... | 24 |
| Queen | ........... | 36 |
| King | ............ | 36 |

**Use the Wheel and Background Fabrics.**

## Making the Wheel/Background

| W | B | W |
|---|---|---|
| B | W | B |

1. Count out 2" strips of **Wheel** fabric and **Background** fabric.

2. Flip the Background strip to the Wheel strip, right sides together.

3. Assembly-line sew the strips together.

4. Press the seams toward the darker fabric.

**Stack and arrange in this order:**

**Stack this many strips:**

| Baby | ....... | 1 of each |
| Lap | ........ | 2 of each |
| Twin | ........ | 6 of each |
| Double | ...... | 6 of each |
| Queen | ..... | 8 of each |
| King | ........ | 8 of each |

**If you choose, layer for faster cutting.**

5. Place the sewn strip on the gridded cutting mat. Trim at zero.

6. Cut pieces **your measurement** of the Four-Patch.

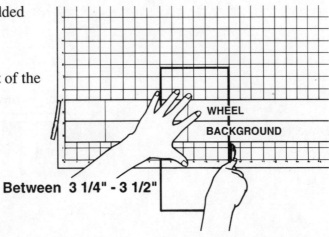

Between 3 1/4" - 3 1/2"

**Cut only this many pieces:**

| Baby | ............ | 8 |
| Lap | ............ | 16 |
| Twin | ........... | 48 |
| Double | .......... | 48 |
| Queen | .......... | 72 |
| King | ............ | 72 |

7. Cut the remaining sewn strips into 2" pieces:

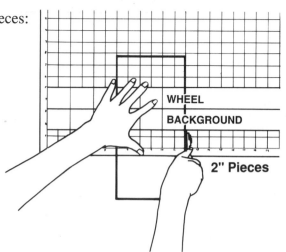

**Cut this many pieces:**

Baby . . . . . . . . . . . . 4
Lap . . . . . . . . . . . . . 8
Twin . . . . . . . . . . 24
Double . . . . . . . . . 24
Queen . . . . . . . . . . 36
King . . . . . . . . . . . 36

8. Arrange the two pieces in this order:

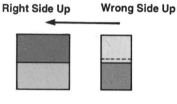

Right Side Up ← Wrong Side Up

9. Place the smaller piece on the larger piece to the left. Wiggle-match the seam.

10. Assembly-line sew.

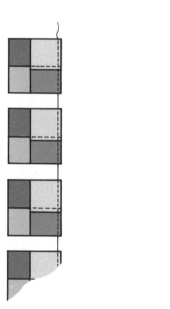

11. Open the sewn together pieces, and arrange. in this order:

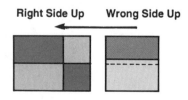

Right Side Up ← Wrong Side Up

12. Place the remaining piece on top.
    Wiggle-match the seam.

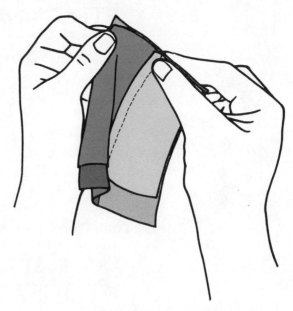

13. Assembly-line sew.

14. Clip the connecting threads.

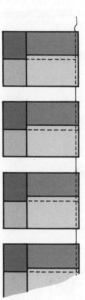

15. From the right side, press the middle
    piece so that the seams fall away from the
    center.

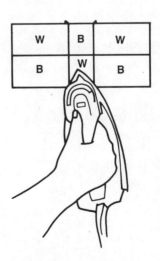

# The Nine-Patch

**Light Background**

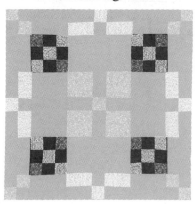

**You need this many:** ⊞

Baby . . . . . . . . . . . . .4

Lap . . . . . . . . . . . . . .8

Twin . . . . . . . . . . . 24

Double . . . . . . . . . .24

Queen . . . . . . . . . . .36

King . . . . . . . . . . . .36

**Dark Background**

**Use the Trail, Wheel, and Background Fabrics.**

## Making the Trail/Background/Wheel

| T | B | W |
|---|---|---|
| W | B | T |

1. Count out 2" strips of **Trail** fabric and **Background** fabric.

2. Assembly-line sew the strips together.

3. Press the seams toward the darker fabric.

**Stack and arrange in this order:**

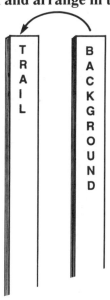

**Stack this many strips:**

Baby . . . . . .1/2 of each

Lap . . . . . . . . 1 of each

Twin . . . . 2 1/2 of each

Double . . 2 1/2 of each

Queen . . . 3 1/2 of each

King . . . . 3 1/2 of each

4. Assembly-line sew a **Wheel** strip to the Background strip.

5. Press the seams toward the darker fabric.

6. Set aside until the next section is completed.

**Add this many strips:**

Baby . . . . . . . . . . .1/2

Lap . . . . . . . . . . . . . .1

Twin . . . . . . . . . 2 1/2

Double . . . . . . . . 2 1/2

Queen . . . . . . . . 3 1/2

King . . . . . . . . . . 3 1/2

# Making the
# Background/Wheel/Background  B W B

1. Count out 2" strips of **Background** fabric and **Wheel** fabric.

2. Assembly-line sew the strips together.

3. Press the seams toward the darker fabric.

**Stack and arrange in this order:**

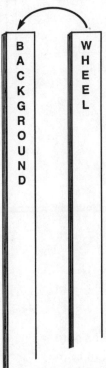

4. Assembly-line sew another **2"** **Background** strip to the Wheel strip.

5. Press the seams toward the darker fabric.

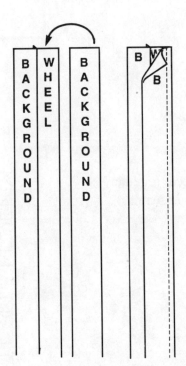

## Layering and Cutting the 2" Paired Pieces

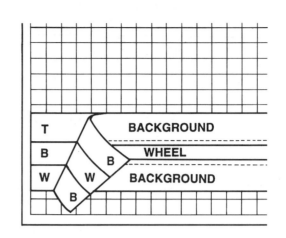

1. Place the Trail/Background/Wheel strip on the gridded cutting mat, right side up. Extend the left end slightly to the left of zero.

2. Place the Background/Wheel/Background strip right sides to it. Lock the center seams.

3. With the 6" x 12" ruler and rotary cutter, trim at zero.

4. Cut paired pieces every 2", carefully lifting and lining up the ruler on the grid.

5. Carefully place the 2" paired pieces onto the Square Up ruler and carry them to the sewing machine.

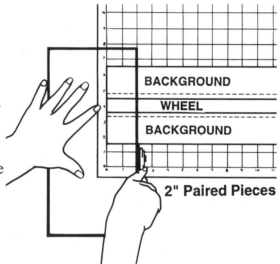

**2" Paired Pieces**

**Cut only this many 2" paired pieces:**

| | |
|---|---|
| Baby | 4 |
| Lap | 8 |
| Twin | 24 |
| Double | 24 |
| Queen | 36 |
| King | 36 |

6. Assembly-line sew the pieces together, as you wiggle-match the center seams.

7. Clip apart.

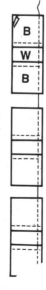

8. Discard the excess Background/Wheel/Background strip.

9. Cut the remaining Trail/Background/Wheel strip into 2" pieces.

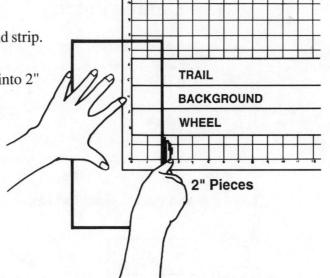

**TRAIL**

**BACKGROUND**

**WHEEL**

**2" Pieces**

10. Stack and arrange in this order:

Right Side Up ← Wrong Side Up

| T | B |
|---|---|
| B | W |
| W | B |

| W |
|---|
| B |
| T |

11. With right sides together, wiggle-match and assembly-line sew into Nine-Patch.

12. Clip the connecting threads.

13. Press the seams away from the center.

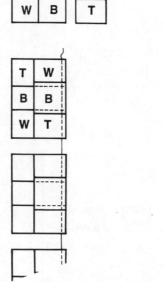

| T | W |
|---|---|
| B | B |
| W | T |

14. Measure several to find an average size.

**Your Nine-Patch measurement will be used when cutting the Lattice strips and Background Pieces.**

*If the seam were a perfect 1/4", the squares would measure 5". However, seam widths and pressing techniques often vary.*

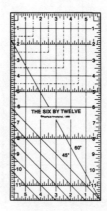

THE SIX BY TWELVE

| T | B | W |
|---|---|---|
| B | W | B |
| W | B | T |

**Circle your measurement:**

**4 1/2"  4 5/8"**

**4 3/4"  4 7/8"  5"**

Light Background

# The Center Patch

You need this many: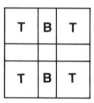

Baby . . . . . . . . . . . . 1

Lap . . . . . . . . . . . . . 2

Twin . . . . . . . . . . . 6

Double . . . . . . . . . . . 6

Queen . . . . . . . . . . . 9

King . . . . . . . . . . . . 9

**Use Trail and Background Fabrics.**

Dark Background

## Making the Trail/Background/Trail

*Strips based on your Four-Patch measurement are now cut from the Trail Fabric.*

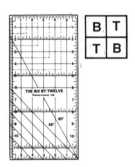

1. Transfer your recorded measurement of the Four-Patch (Page 28), between 3 1/4" and 3 1/2". _____ "

2. From the **Trail fabric**, cut strips your Four-Patch measurement from selvage to selvage.

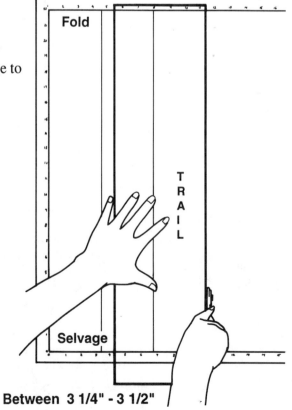

**Fold**

**T R A I L**

**Selvage**

**Between 3 1/4" - 3 1/2"**

**Cut this many Trail strips:**

Baby . . . . . . . . . . . 1/2

Lap . . . . . . . . . . . . . . 1

Twin . . . . . . . . . . . . . 2

Double . . . . . . . . . . . 2

Queen . . . . . . . . . . . . 3

King . . . . . . . . . . . . . 3

*Cut one of the above strips in half for Baby, Lap, Queen, and King.*

3. Count out these **Trail** fabric strips with previously cut **2" Background** strips.

4. Sew together.

**Stack and arrange in this order:**

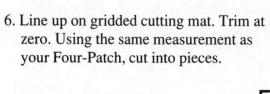

```
T          B          T
R          A          R
A          C          A
I          K          I
L          G          L
           R
           O
           U
           N
           D
```

**Stack this many strips:**

Baby . . . . . . 1/4 of each
Lap . . . . . . . 1/2 of each
Twin . . . . . . . 1 of each
Double . . . . . 1 of each
Queen . . . 1 1/2 of each
King . . . . 1 1/2 of each

5. Press the seams toward the darker fabric.

6. Line up on gridded cutting mat. Trim at zero. Using the same measurement as your Four-Patch, cut into pieces.

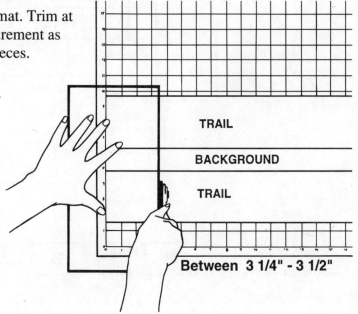

TRAIL

BACKGROUND

TRAIL

Between 3 1/4" - 3 1/2"

**Cut this many pieces:**

Baby . . . . . . . . . . . . . 2
Lap . . . . . . . . . . . . . . 4
Twin . . . . . . . . . . . . 12
Double . . . . . . . . . . 12
Queen . . . . . . . . . . . 18
King . . . . . . . . . . . . . 18

## Making the
## Background/Trail/Background

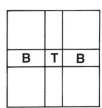

**Baby and Lap Only**

1. From a remaining **2" Background strip**, cut pieces the same measurement as your Four-Patch.

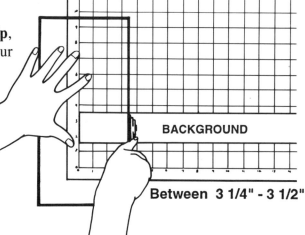

Baby .......... cut 2
Lap ........... cut 4

2. From a remaining **2" Trail strip**, cut 2" squares.

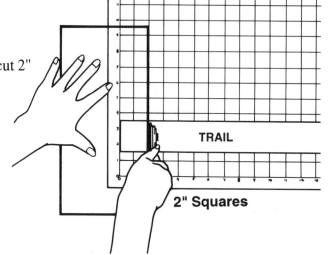

Baby .......... cut 1
Lap ........... cut 2

3. Sew together.
4. Press the seams toward the darker fabric.

| B | T | B |

Baby ............. 1
Lap .............. 2

# Twin, Double, Queen and King

1. Cut **one strip** selvage to selvage from the **Background** fabric using your Four-Patch measurement.

2. Cut the one strip in half.

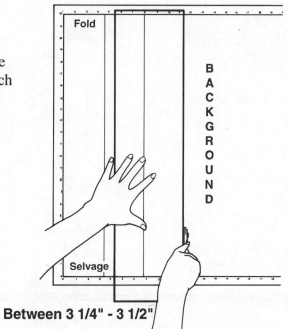

**Between 3 1/4" - 3 1/2"**

3. Arrange the Background half strips with a **2" Trail** strip cut in half in this order:

4. Sew together.

5. Press the seams toward the darker fabric.

6. Cut into 2" pieces.

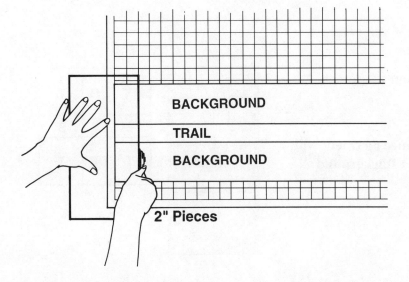

**2" Pieces**

**Cut this many pieces:**

Twin . . . . . . . . . . . . . .6
Double . . . . . . . . . . . .6
Queen . . . . . . . . . . . . .9
King . . . . . . . . . . . . . .9

**Making the**

| T | B | T |
|---|---|---|
| B | T | B |
| T | B | T |

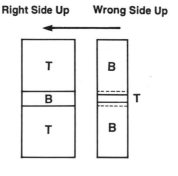

**Right Side Up**  **Wrong Side Up**

1. Arrange equal stacks in this order:

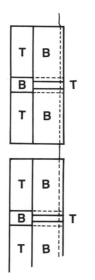

2. Place the smaller piece on the larger piece to the left. Wiggle-match seams.

3. Assembly-line sew.

4. Assembly-line sew the remaining piece to the sewn pair.

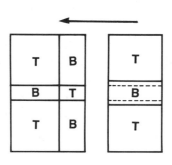

5. Clip the connecting threads.

6. Press the seams toward the darker fabric.

7. Measure several to find an average measurement.

   **Your Center Patch measurement will be used when cutting Background Pieces.**

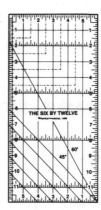

| T | B | T |
|---|---|---|
| B | T | B |
| T | B | T |

Circle your measurement:

7 1/2"    7 5/8"

7 3/4"    7 7/8"    8"

40

Light Background

# The Background Pieces

Dark Background

### Use the Background Fabric.

There are **three different sizes of pieces** all cut from Background strips the width of your Nine-Patch.  The **first is the Lattice**, longer than half a strip and width the same measurement as your Nine-Patch.

The **other two are pieces within the block**. Their measurements are based on your sizes of the Center Patch and Four-Patch.

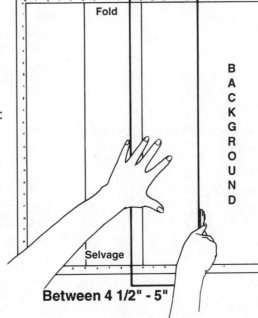

Fold

BACKGROUND

Selvage

**Between 4 1/2" - 5"**

## Cutting the Background Strips

1. Transfer your recorded measurement of the Nine-Patch (page 35), between 4 1/2" and 5":

_____"

2. Cut strips your measurement from selvage to selvage.

**Cut this many strips:**

Baby . . . . . . . . . . . . .4
Lap . . . . . . . . . . . . . .7
Twin . . . . . . . . . . . .17
Double . . . . . . . . . .17
Queen . . . . . . . . . .24
King . . . . . . . . . . . .24

## Cutting the Lattice from Background Strips

1. Unfold the strips and layer on the gridded cutting mat with the selvage ends extending slightly to the left of zero.

2. Layer cut at zero, trimming off the selvages.

3. Layer cut Lattice strips at 24". This is approximately 1" longer than the estimated size of your sewn together block.

4. Set the Lattice aside until the block is sewn together.

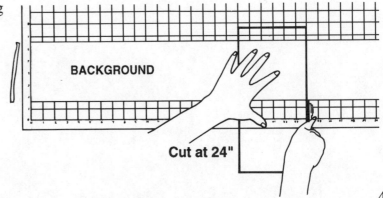

BACKGROUND

**Cut at 24"**

*The excess is now cut into the two smaller pieces needed to sew the block together.*

## Cutting the Two Pieces from the Excess Background Strip

1. Transfer your measurements, referring to the pages indicated:

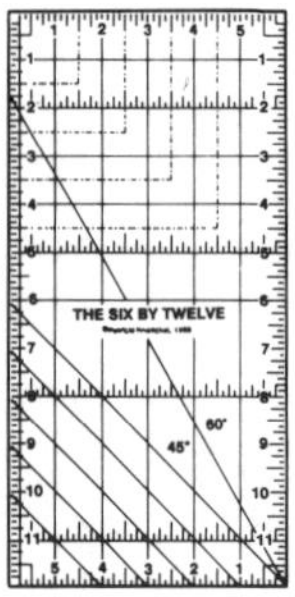

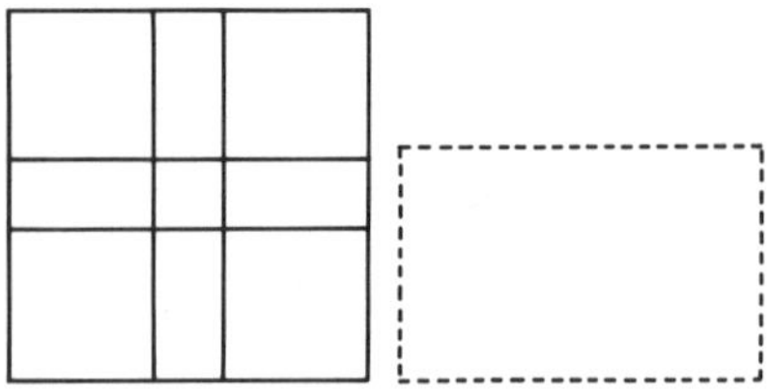

   **Center Patch (page 40)** _____ "

   Between 7 1/2" - 8"

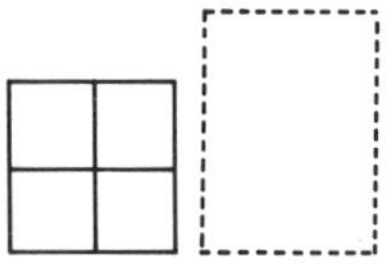

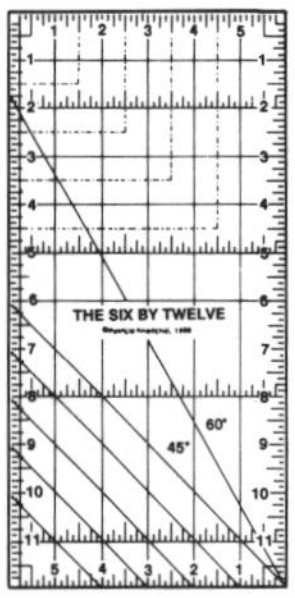

   This is your length of the **larger** piece.

   **Four-Patch (page 28)** _____ "

   Between 3 1/4" - 3 1/2"

   This is your length of the **smaller** piece.

2. Cut **one** Background strip into these two lengths to check your measurements.

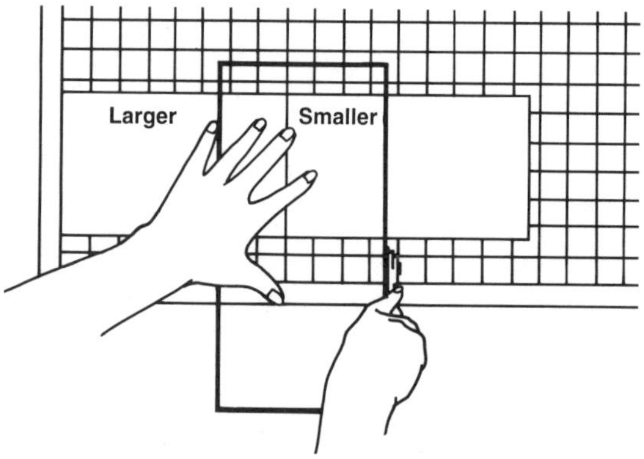

   Larger   Smaller

3. Lay out your finished patches. Check the test pieces against the empty spaces.

4. Once the measurements are correct, layer cut the Background strips into these pieces. The smaller pieces may be cut from the scraps.

**Cut this many Larger pieces:**

| | |
|---|---|
| Baby | 4 |
| Lap | 8 |
| Twin | 24 |
| Double | 24 |
| Queen | 36 |
| King | 36 |

**Cut this many Smaller pieces:**

| | |
|---|---|
| Baby | 8 |
| Lap | 16 |
| Twin | 48 |
| Double | 48 |
| Queen | 72 |
| King | 72 |

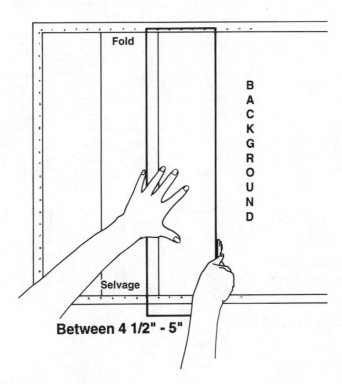

5. You may need to cut additional strips the width of the Nine-Patch from the Background fabric for the total number of pieces.

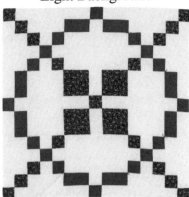

Light Background

# Sewing the Block Together

Dark Background

**Use all Patches and Background Pieces.**

## Laying out the Block

1. Lay out the pieces for one block in an area at least 24" square to the right of your sewing machine.

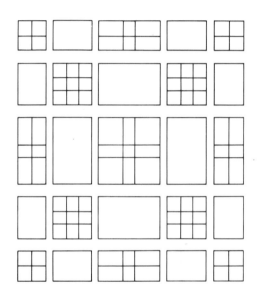

2. Flip the second vertical row right sides together to the first vertical row.

3. Stack rows from bottom to top, so the top piece is on the top of the stack.

4. Assembly-line sew the first two vertical rows, matching the pieces and butting them close together. Backstitch the outside edges. Sew over the seams as they were pressed. Do not clip apart.

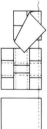
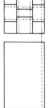
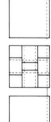

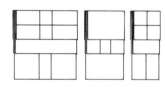

44

5. Open the pieces, and flip the third row right sides together to the second row as you assembly-line sew.

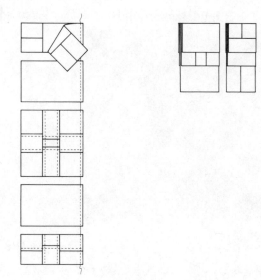

6. Assembly-line sew the fourth and fifth vertical rows. Do not clip the threads.

7. Check block placement before going on.

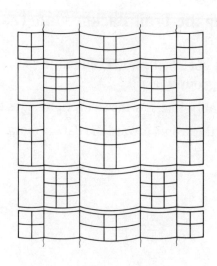

8. Sew the horizontal rows, always matching the seams and pushing them in opposite directions, toward the darker when possible.

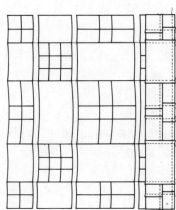

9. From the wrong side, press the seams flat.

10. Measure the block and record the measurement.

_____"

11. Sew all the blocks in this order.

Light Background

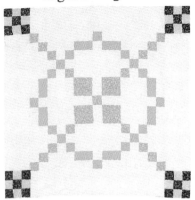

# The Cornerstone

**You need this many:** ⊞

| | |
|---|---|
| Baby | . . . . . . . . . . . . 4 |
| Lap | . . . . . . . . . . . . . 6 |
| Twin | . . . . . . . . . . . . 12 |
| Double | . . . . . . . . . . 12 |
| Queen | . . . . . . . . . . . 16 |
| King | . . . . . . . . . . . . 16 |

Dark Background

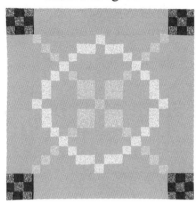

**Use the Trail and Background Fabrics.**

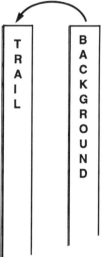

## Making the Trail/Background/Trail

1. Count out 2" strips of **Trail** fabric and **Background** fabric.

2. Assembly-line sew the strips right sides together.

3. Press the seams toward the darker fabric.

**Stack this many strips:**

| | |
|---|---|
| Baby | . . . . . . 1/2 of each |
| Lap | . . . . . . . . 1 of each |
| Twin | . . . . 1 1/4 of each |
| Double | . . 1 1/4 of each |
| Queen | . . . . . . 2 of each |
| King | . . . . . . . 2 of each |

**Stack and arrange in this order:**

4. Assembly-line sew a matching **Trail** strip to the Background strip.

5. Press the seams toward the darker fabric.

6. Set aside until the next section is completed.

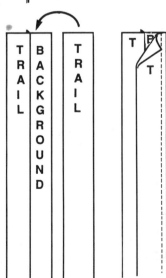

**Add this many strips:**

| | |
|---|---|
| Baby | . . . . . . . . . . . 1/2 |
| Lap | . . . . . . . . . . . . . 1 |
| Twin | . . . . . . . . . . 1 1/4 |
| Double | . . . . . . . . . 1 1/4 |
| Queen | . . . . . . . . . . . 2 |
| King | . . . . . . . . . . . . 2 |

# Making the Background/Trail/Background

1. Count out 2" strips of **Background** fabric and **Trail** fabric.
2. Assembly-line sew the strips right sides together.
3. Press the seams toward the darker fabric.

**Arrange in this order:**

4. Assembly-line sew a matching **Background** strip to the Trail strip.
5. Press the seams toward the darker fabric.

**Stack this many strips:**

| | |
|---|---|
| Baby | 1/4 of each |
| Lap | 1/2 of each |
| Twin | 1 of each |
| Double | 1 of each |
| Queen | 1 of each |
| King | 1 of each |

**Add this many strips:**

| | |
|---|---|
| Baby | 1/4 |
| Lap | 1/2 |
| Twin | 1 |
| Double | 1 |
| Queen | 1 |
| King | 1 |

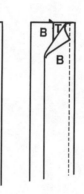

## Layering and Cutting the 2" Paired Pieces

1. Place the Trail/Background/Trail strip on the gridded cutting mat, right side up. Extend the left end slightly to the left of zero.
2. Place the Background/Trail/Background strip right sides to it. Wiggle-match the center seams.

3. With the 6" x 12" ruler and rotary cutter, layer cut at zero.
4. Layer cut every 2", carefully lifting and lining up the ruler on the grid.
5. Carefully place the 2" paired pieces on the ruler.

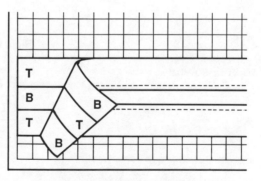

**2" Paired Pieces**

**Layer cut this many 2" paired pieces:**

| | |
|---|---|
| Baby | 4 |
| Lap | 6 |
| Twin | 12 |
| Double | 12 |
| Queen | 16 |
| King | 16 |

6. Wiggle-match the center seams as you assembly-line sew the pieces together.

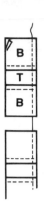

7. Separate the two layers of strips. Discard the excess Background/Trail/Background strip.

8. Cut the remaining Trail/Background/Trail strips into 2" pieces.

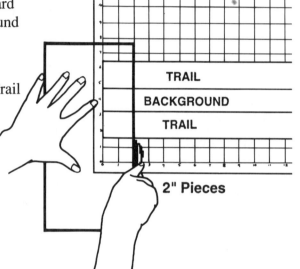

TRAIL

BACKGROUND

TRAIL

2" Pieces

**Cut this many 2" pieces:**
Baby . . . . . . . . . . . . . 4
Lap . . . . . . . . . . . . . . 6
Twin . . . . . . . . . . . . .12
Double . . . . . . . . . . .12
Queen . . . . . . . . . . . .16
King . . . . . . . . . . . . .16

9. Place the stacks next to your sewing machine in this order:

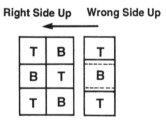

Right Side Up      Wrong Side Up

| T | B | T |
| B | T | B |
| T | B | T |

10. With right sides together, wiggle-match and assembly-line sew into nine-patch.

11. Clip the connecting threads. Press the seams away from the center.

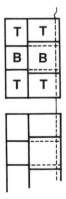

| T | T |
| B | B |
| T | T |

# Sewing the Quilt Top Together

Light Background

Dark Background

**Use the 24" Lattice strips of Background fabric.**

## Cutting the Lattice to Block Size

1. Cut the Background fabric into Lattice the length of your sewn together block.

   Refer to page 45 for measurement.

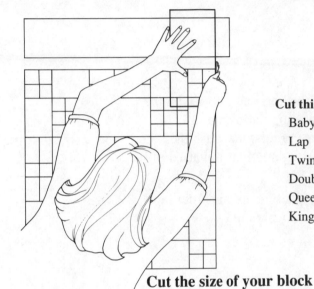

**Cut this many:**
- Baby . . . . . . . . . . . . 4
- Lap . . . . . . . . . . . . 7
- Twin . . . . . . . . . . . 17
- Double . . . . . . . . . . 17
- Queen . . . . . . . . . . 24
- King . . . . . . . . . . . . 24

**Cut the size of your block**

2. Press a crease across midpoint on each Lattice.

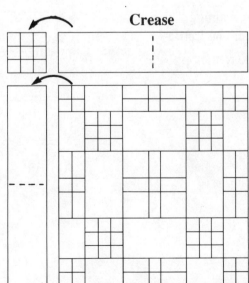

3. Place the Lattice, one Cornerstone, and one block in this order to the right of your sewing machine:

**Crease**

**Crease**

4. Flip the horizontal Lattice right sides together to the Cornerstone. Match the outside edges and sew the two together.

5. Flip the block right sides together to the vertical Lattice. Pin the midpoint crease in the Lattice to the center of the block. Pin the outside edges.

6. Sew across the seams as they were pressed.

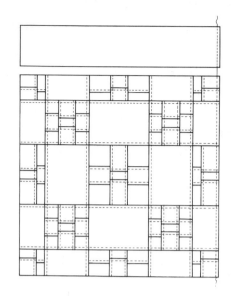

7. Turn, and sew the horizontal row with the block on top, sewing the seams as pressed. At the cornerstone, push the seams in opposite directions toward the darker fabric.

8. Sew one block at a time in this order.

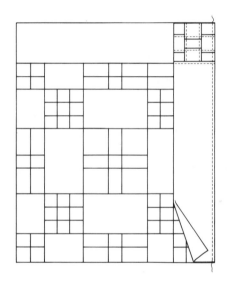

9. Assembly-line sew the remaining Cornerstones to the remaining Lattice.

10. Sew the last Cornerstone to the opposite side of the last Lattice.

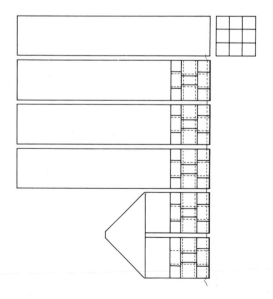

11. Lay out your quilt in rows following your particular diagram.

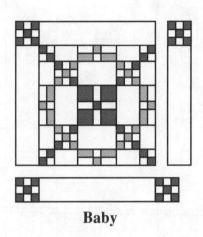

**Baby**

**Lap**

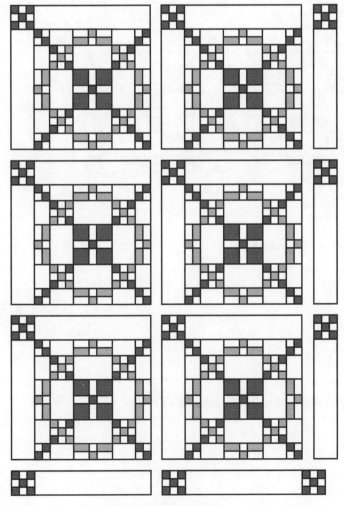

**Twin and Double**

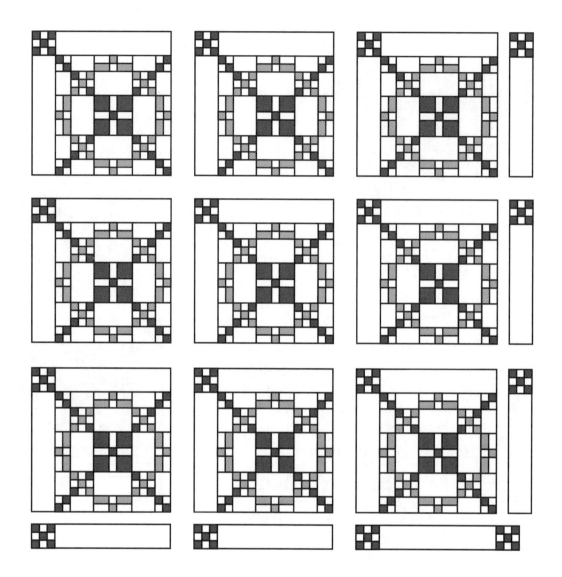

**Queen and King**

12. Set the blocks together into rows in the larger quilts.

13. Add a Lattice and Cornerstone to the end of each row.

14. Sew the rows together.

15. Sew the bottom row of Lattice and Cornerstones together. Sew to the quilt top.

# Designing Your Borders

Be creative when adding borders. Suggested border yardage and border examples are given for each quilt. However, you may wish to custom design the borders by changing the widths of the strips. This might change backing and batting yardage.

When custom fitting the quilt, lay the top on your bed before adding the borders and backing. Measure to find how much border is needed to get the fit you want. Keep in mind that the quilt will "shrink" approximately 3" in the length and width after tying, "stitching in the ditch," and/or machine quilting.

## Piecing the Border and Optional Binding Strips

1. Stack and square off the ends of each strip, trimming away the selvage edges.
2. Seam the strips of each fabric into long pieces by assembly-line sewing. Lay the first strip right side up. Lay the second strip right sides to it. Backstitch, stitch the short ends together, and backstitch again.

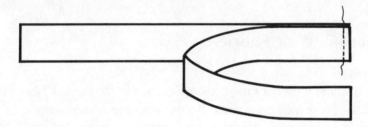

3. Take the strip on the top and fold it so the right side is up.
4. Place the third strip right sides to it, backstitch, stitch, and backstitch again.

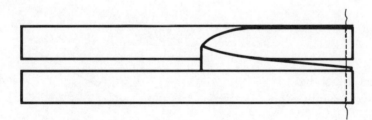

5. Continue assembly-line sewing all the short ends together into long pieces for each fabric.
6. Clip the threads holding the strips together.

## Sewing the Borders to the Quilt Top

1. Measure down the center to find the length.

2. Cut two strips that measurement from the First Border fabric. Square off each end with the rotary cutter and ruler as you cut.

3. Pin in the center and then to each side, easing or stretching as needed. Sew. Fold out and flat. Press away from the quilt top.

4. Measure across the center to find the width, including the first borders.

5. Cut two strips that measurement. Square off the ends as you cut.

6. Pin to top and bottom, easing or stretching as needed. Sew. Fold out and flat. All borders are added in this manner.

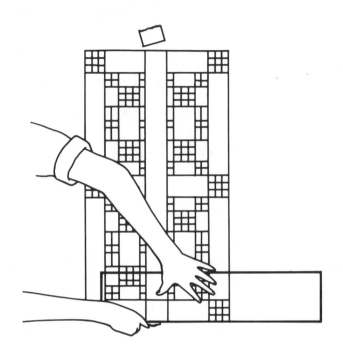

## Preparing the Backing from 44" Wide Fabric

1. Following your Cutting Chart, fold the long backing crosswise and cut into equal pieces. If you custom fitted your quilt, you may need to adjust these measurements. If your backing is too narrow, use your leftover fabrics, and add a section down the middle. If your backing is too short, add a strip to each end from leftovers.

2. Tear off the selvages and seam the backing pieces together.

3. Embroider your name and date on the backing with hand stitching or machine writing. Consider adding your state as many quilts travel across the country.

## Piecing the Bonded Batting

1. If the batting needs to be pieced to get the desired size, cut and butt the two straight edges closely without overlapping.

2. Whipstitch the edges together with a double strand of thread. Do not pull the threads tightly as this will create a hard ridge visible on the outside of the quilt.

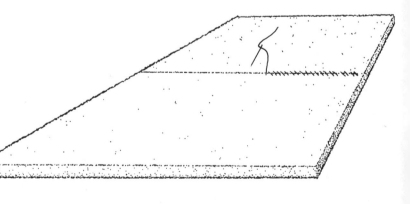

# Two Different Methods of Finishing

## 1. Quick Turn Method

The first method, the Quick Turn, is the easier and faster way of finishing the quilt. Thick batting is "rolled" into the middle of the quilt, and the layers are held together with ties. Borders may be "stitched in the ditch" for additional dimension.

## 2. Machine Quilting and Binding Method (Page 59)

In the second method, the three layers of backing, batting and quilt top are machine quilted and bound with a straight grain strip of binding. A thin batting is used for ease in quilting.

## Quick Turn Method

1. Lay out the backing fabric, right side up, on a large table or floor. Clamp to the table with binder clips or tape to the floor.

2. Lay the quilt top on the backing fabric with right sides together. Stretch and smooth the top. Pin. Trim away excess backing. They should be the same size.

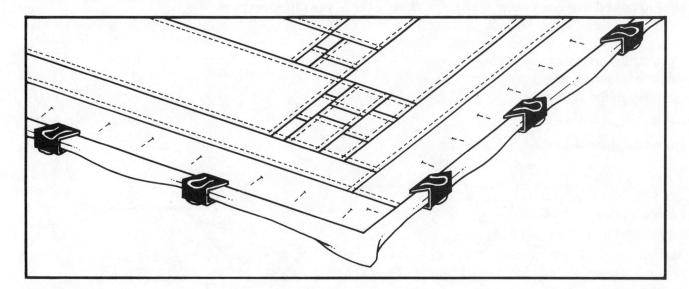

3. Stitch around the four sides of the quilt, leaving a 24" opening in the middle of one long side. Do not turn the quilt right side out.

4. Lay the quilt on top of the batting. Smooth and trim the batting to the same size as the quilt top.

5. To assure that the batting stays out to the edges, whipstitch the batting to the 1/4" seam allowance around the outside edge of the quilt.

## Turning the Quilt Top

One person can turn the quilt alone, but it's helpful if two or three others can help. Read this whole section before beginning.

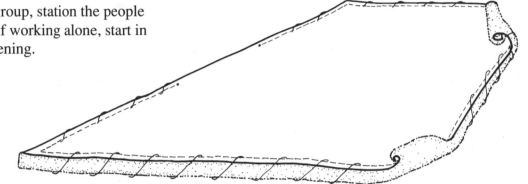

1. If you are working with a group, station the people at the corners of the quilt. If working alone, start in one corner opposite the opening.

2. Roll the corners and sides tightly to keep the batting in place as you roll toward the opening.

**If several people are helping, all should roll toward the opening. If only one is doing the rolling, use a knee to hold down one corner while stretching over to the other corners.**

3. Open up the opening over this huge wad of fabric and batting, and pop the quilt right side out through the hole.

4. Unroll carefully with the layers together.

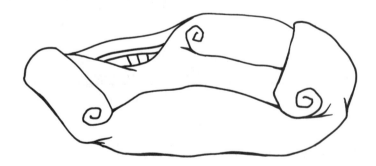

5. Lay the quilt flat on the floor or on a very large table. Work out all wrinkles and bumps by stationing two people opposite each other around the quilt. Have each person grasp the edge and tug the quilt in opposite directions.

6. You can also relocate any batting by reaching inside the quilt through the opening with a yardstick. Hold the edges and shake the batting into place if necessary.

7. Slipstitch the opening shut.

## Finishing the Quick Turn Quilt

You may choose to tie your entire quilt, or machine quilt by "stitching in the ditch" around the borders and tying in the blocks.

A thick batting is difficult to machine quilt except for the borders, as it is hard to get all the rolled thickness to fit through the keyhole of the sewing machine.

## Tying the Quilt

1. Thread a large-eyed curved needle with six strands of embroidery floss, crochet thread, or other thread of your choice.

2. Plan where you want your ties placed. You may choose to tie at the corners of each patch, accenting the Trail and Wheel design.

   Do not tie in the borders if you wish to "stitch in the ditch."

3. Starting in the center of the quilt and working to the outside, take a 1/4" stitch through all thicknesses at the points you wish to tie. Draw the curved needle along to each point, going in and out, and replacing the tying material as needed.

4. Clip all the stitches midway.

5. Tie the strands into surgeon's square knots by taking the strand on the right and wrapping it twice. Pull the knot tight. Take the strand on the left, wrap it twice, and pull the knot tight.

6. Clip the strands so they are 1/2" to 1" long.

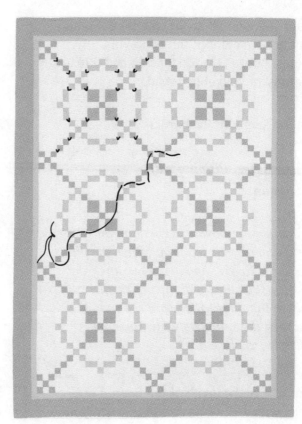

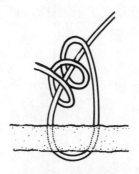

**Right over left and wrap twice.**

**Pull tight.**

**Left over right and wrap twice.**

**Pull tight.**

## Stitching in the Ditch

For more dimensional borders, you many choose to "stitch in the ditch" rather than tie the borders. A walking foot or even-feed foot sewing machine attachment is necessary to keep the three layers feeding at the same rate.

1. Change your stitch length to 10 stitches per inch. Match your bobbin color of thread to your backing color. Loosen the top tension and thread with the soft nylon invisible thread.

2. **Safety pin** the length of the borders.

*Quick and Easy Safety Pinning with a Grapefruit Spoon*

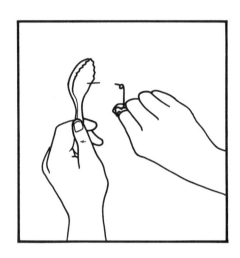

*Grasp the opened pin in your right hand and the grape fruit spoon in your left hand. Push the pin through the three layers, and bring the tip of the pin back out. Just as the tip of the pin surfaces, catch the tip in the serrated edge of the spoon. Twist the side of the spoon up while pushing down on the pin, to close it.*

3. Place the needle in the depth of the seam. Lock your threads with 1/8" of tiny stitches when you begin and end your sewing. Run your hand underneath to feel for puckers. Grasp the quilt with your left hand above the sewing machine, and grasp the quilt ten inches below the walking foot with your right hand as you stitch. If you need to ease in the top fabric, feed the quilt through the machine by pushing the layers of fabric and batting forward underneath the walking foot.

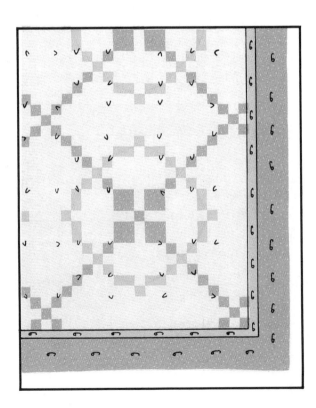

If puckering occurs, remove stitching by grasping the bobbin thread with a pin or tweezers and pull gently to expose the invisible thread. Touch the invisible thread stitches with the rotary cutter blade as you pull the bobbin thread free from the quilt.

4. Remove safety pins and store in opened position.

# Machine Quilting and Binding Method

Be creative when deciding what to machine quilt.

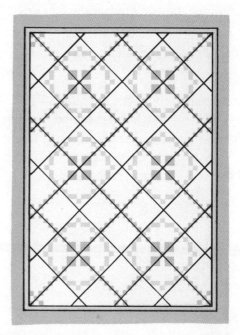

You may choose to "stitch in the ditch" through the seams of the lattice and cornerstones.

Or you may choose diagonal stitching through and between the Trail pieces.

## Adding the Backing and Batting

1. Stretch out the backing right side down on a large floor area or table. Tape down on a floor area or clamp onto a table with large binder clips.

2. Place and smooth out the batting on top. Lay the quilt top right side up and centered on top of the batting. Completely smooth and stretch all layers until they are flat. Tape or clip securely. The backing and batting should extend at least 2" on all sides.

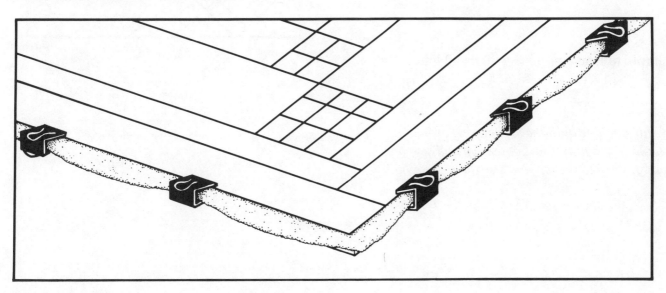

3. With the 6" x 24" ruler and marking pencil, lightly mark the diagonal lines for machine quilting. *Use chalk, a thin dry sliver of soap, or a silver pencil for marking. Make certain that you can remove the marks from the fabric.*

   Chalk lines are not necessary when stitching through the seams in the lattice and cornerstones.

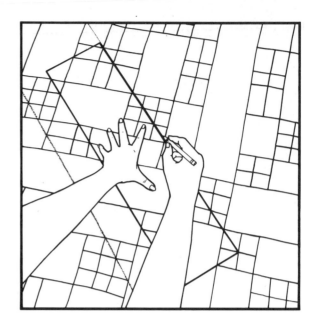

4. Place safety pins throughout the quilt away from lines where you will be machine quilting. Begin pinning in the center and work to the outside. They should be spaced every 5". See page 58 for safety pinning technique.

5. Trim the backing and batting to within 2" of the outside edge of the quilt.

6. Roll the quilt tightly from the outside edge in toward the middle. *Roll on the diagonal for quilting through the Trail. Roll on the straight for quilting through the lattice.* Hold this roll with metal bicycle clips or pins.

7. Slide this roll into the keyhole of the sewing machine.

8. Machine quilt or "stitch in the ditch" on the line or in the depth of the seam. See page 58.

   *Use invisible thread in the top of your machine and regular thread in the bobbin to match the backing. Loosen the top tension, and lengthen your stitch to 8 - 10 stitches per inch, or a # 4.*

9. Unroll, roll, and machine quilt on all lines.

*If you machine quilt the Wheel, sew around it one-half at a time. Start at the top and sew one half. Return to the top and sew the second half.*

# Adding the Binding

**Use a walking foot attachment and regular thread on top and in the bobbin to match the binding. Use 10 stitches per inch.**

1. Press the binding strip in half lengthwise with right sides out.

2. Line up the raw edges of the folded binding with the raw edges of the quilt in the middle of one side.

3. Begin stitching 4" from the end of the binding.

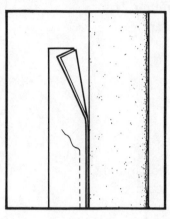

4. At the corner, stop the stitching 1/4" from the edge with the needle in the fabric. Raise the presser foot and turn the quilt to the next side. Put the foot back down.

5. Stitch backwards 1/4" to the edge of the binding, raise the foot, and pull the quilt forward slightly.

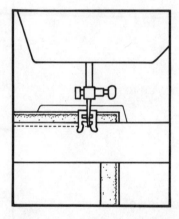

6. Fold the binding strip straight up on the diagonal. Fingerpress in the diagonal fold.

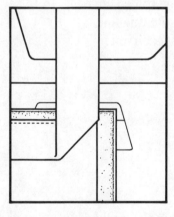

7. Fold the binding strip straight down with the diagonal fold underneath. Line up the top of the fold with the raw edge of the binding underneath.

8. Begin stitching from the corner.

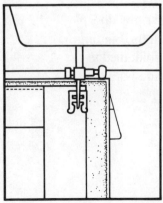

9. Continue stitching and mitering the corners around the outside of the quilt.

10. Stop stitching 4" from where the ends will overlap.

11. Line up the two ends of binding. Trim the excess with a 1/2" overlap.

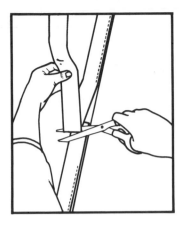

12. Open out the folded ends and pin right sides together. Sew a 1/4" seam.

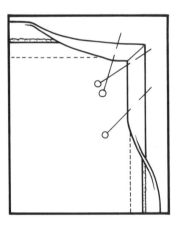

13. Continue to stitch the binding in place.

14. Trim the batting and backing up to the raw edges of the binding.

15. Fold the binding to the backside of the quilt. Pin in place so that the folded edge on the binding covers the stitching line. Tuck in the excess fabric at each miter on the diagonal.

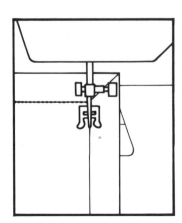

16. From the right side, "stitch in the ditch" using invisible thread on the right side, and a bobbin thread to match the binding on the back side. Catch the folded edge of the binding on the back side with the stitching.

# Index

# Order Information:

If you do not have a quilt shop in your area, you may write for a complete catalog and current price list of all books and patterns published by Quilt in a Day® Inc.

## Books

Quilt in a Day Log Cabin
The Sampler -- A Machine Sewn Quilt
Trio of Treasured Quilts
Lover's Knot Quilt
Amish Quilt in a Day
Irish Chain in a Day
Country Christmas
Bunnies and Blossoms
May Basket Quilt
Diamond Log Cabin Tablecloth or Treeskirt
Morning Star Quilt
Trip Around the World Quilt
Friendship Quilt
Creating With Color
Dresden Plate Quilt, A Simplified Method
Pineapple Quilt, a Piece of Cake
Radiant Star Quilt
Blazing Star Tablecloth
Tulip Quilt
Scrap Quilt, Strips and Spider Webs
Block Party Series I
     Quilter's Year
Block Party Series II
     Baskets & Flowers
Block Party Series III
     Quilters' Almanac

## Booklets and Patterns

Patchwork Santa
Last Minute Gifts
Dresden Plate Placemats and Tea Cozy
Angel of Antiquity
Log Cabin Wreath Wallhanging
Log Cabin Christmas Tree Wallhanging
Flying Geese Quilt
Miniature May Basket Wallhanging
Tulip Table Runner and Wallhanging
Heart's Delight, Nine-Patch Variations
Country Flag Wallhanging
Spools and Tools Wallhanging
Schoolhouse Wallhanging

## Videos

Log Cabin Video
Lover's Knot Video
Irish Chain Video
Ohio Star Video
Blazing Star Video
Scrap Quilt Video
Morning Star Video
Trip around the World Video
Pineapple Video
Radiant Star Video
Flying Geese Video
. . . . and many others

If you are ever in San Diego County, southern California, drop by the Quilt in a Day Center quilt shop and classroom in the La Costa Meadows Business Park. Write ahead for a current class schedule and map.

Eleanor Burns may be seen on Educational Public Broadcasting Stations (PBS) throughout the country. Check your TV listing in your area for dates and times.

## Quilt in a Day® Inc.

1955 Diamond Street, San Marcos, California 92069

Phone: 1(800) U2 KWILT (1-800-825-9458) Information Line: 1(619) 591-0081